What Can You Do to Receive From God?

EXPECT

Kenneth W. Hagin

Expect
ISBN-13: 978-0-89276-757-1
ISBN-10: 0-89276-757-X

Copyright © 2016 by Rhema Bible Church
AKA Kenneth Hagin Ministries, Inc.
All rights reserved.
Printed in USA

In the U.S. write:
Kenneth Hagin Ministries
P.O. Box 50126
Tulsa, OK 74150-0126
1-888-28-FAITH
rhema.org

In Canada, write:
Kenneth Hagin Ministries
P.O. Box 335, Station D
Etobicoke (Toronto), Ontario
Canada, M9A 4X3
1-866-70-RHEMA
rhemacanada.org

Contents

Introduction

Dreams are a preview of the possibilities you can have in life. Jesus said in Mark 9:23 (NIV), *"Everything is possible for one who believes."* I believe God wants you to have a full life—a life where you see the reality of your dreams and you experience everything that He has promised you in Scripture.

Let me ask you three questions.

What is the biggest thing you think God can do? Most people would say, "There's no limit. God can do anything."

Then, what is the biggest thing you think God can do for *you*? This brings it a little closer to home. Your answer can't be so general. Yes, God can do anything, but what will He do for *you*?

Finally, what is the biggest thing you think God can do for you *today*? This puts your answer in the *now*.

I've asked these questions because I want you to realize something: Too often, people are vague in their thoughts about God, His abundance, and what He'll do for them.

It's easy to give general answers about what God can do. But when we start thinking about what He can do for us today, we can't be so ambiguous. That's when we start to squirm a little bit!

You see, many Christians are struggling with lack, sickness, and many other things. They've become disillusioned in their faith because they're not experiencing what God's Word says they can have.

Some people have been disappointed time and time again. When they talk, you can hear hopelessness in their voices and see despondence in their eyes. They are just going through the motions. They get up in the morning, go to work, come home, and go to bed. They do this over and over again. This is their life.

Adversity has taken them to a point where they don't believe that possibilities even exist. They've become blinded to the truth that their situation can change.

I've seen people become so disheartened that they've stopped dreaming. They've lost all hope and don't believe their situation can turn around. I've heard them say, "Can anything good come out of this?"

We've all had our dreams and desires crushed on the rocks of adversity. But we often fail to realize that people who've experienced great success have also experienced many setbacks and disappointments. Instead of quitting, these men and women kept seeing possibilities. They kept moving forward. This is something we should all strive to do.

Remember, no matter how disappointed we become or how bad everything looks, possibilities still exist. In fact, they're right where we are. They're in the middle of our worst nightmare and even in the midst of our greatest victories.

It can be hard to see possibilities when we're surrounded by adversity because everything seems so bleak. But the same thing can happen when we experience a great victory. Sometimes people think all of their victories have been won and there's nothing more to achieve. This is not true—there are more victories to go after!

God created us with the ability to dream. Actually, *dreams are seeds for our future.* They are a preview of the possibilities that exist for us.

When we start a new job, we dream of the possibility of promotion. When we go to a college or university, we dream of what that education can do for us.

For a dream to become reality, we have to *expect* it to happen. We have to see it *before* it happens. My dad, Kenneth E. Hagin, used to tell people all the time, "See yourself healed." This was an important step for them to receive their healing.

Start seizing your dreams! See yourself accomplishing the things you've always dreamed of, whether they are in the natural realm or the spiritual. Remember, the size of your dream determines the greatness of your future.

My dad used to tell me all the time to dream big. "Set your goals high. Don't set them low," he would say. "If you set your goals high and reach half of them, you've accomplished something. But if you set them low and reach all of them, you haven't done anything."

Woodrow Wilson, the 28th president of the United States, said, "We grow great by dreams. All big men are dreamers. They see things in the soft haze of a spring day or in the red fire of a long winter's evening. Some of us let these dreams die, but others nourish and protect them; nurse them through bad days till they bring them to the sunshine and light which comes always to those who sincerely hope that their dreams will come true."[1]

Are you a dreamer? Do you have dreams? Hold on to them and never give them up. What you want so badly *is* possible. So stop wishing you were somewhere else and start looking for the possibilities that exist right where you are.

One thing is sure: God knows that possibilities exist for income, employment, promotion, favor, and whatever else you want or need. Instead of looking at your circumstances, look to your Heavenly Father. Rely on Him to help you in your situation. Expect Him to move on your behalf.

Expectation is a vital ingredient in your faith walk. Faith is the switch that activates God's power. But if you're not expecting anything, your faith will become stagnant.

EXPECT

In this book I focus on the importance of expectation. Lack of it will keep you bound in a life that is far below what God has provided in His Word. But keeping your focus on the Lord in expectant faith is what you can do to receive from Him!

---

[1]goodreads.com/quotes/179441-we-grow-great-by-dreams-all-big-men-are-dreamers

How to Use This Book

My favorite verse of scripture is Luke 18:27, *"The things which are impossible with men are possible with God."* Over the years, I have faced seemingly impossible situations. But time and again, God has turned them around.

Our Heavenly Father is not a respecter of persons (Acts 10:34). What He did for me, He will do for you. This book was written to help you receive what you have been standing for in faith—those things that may seem impossible to obtain.

Helpful study questions are included at the end of each chapter. You can work on the material by yourself, but I feel that you will benefit more if you go through this book with a study group. Together, you can encourage each other to stand strong in faith.

Each chapter contains the following:

Scriptures to Ponder

These scriptures support the teaching in each chapter. It's a good idea to meditate on these verses until your heart is grounded in them.

Power Points

These are concise summaries of the main points of each chapter.

Just Sayin', Proclaim Your Victory!

These are short confessions you can make to declare the truth of God's Word.

EXPECT

Action Items

These are steps you can take to help you receive what you are believing God for.

1
Good or Bad, You'll Have What You Expect

What are you expecting?

Anything? Something good? Or do you believe that if anything bad is going to happen, it will happen to you?

When my dad, Kenneth E. Hagin, pastored, the services almost always ended with everybody coming to the altar to pray. Dad often walked among the people, tapped them on the shoulder, and asked, "What are you praying about?"

"Nothing in particular," was the reply he heard most often.

"Then that's what you'll get—nothing in particular!" he'd tell them.

Prayer involves expectation. If you expect something, you believe it will happen. When you pray, you first expect God to hear you. Then you expect Him to move on your behalf. On the other hand, if you're not expecting anything, that's exactly what you'll get—nothing!

Expectation Is a Driving Force

Earl Nightingale, an American radio personality in the 1950s, said, "We tend to live up to our expectations."[1] In other words, what you expect is usually how your life goes.

For example, in the springtime, a farmer prepares the fields by plowing the soil and adding manure or other fertilizer and compost. Then he plants seed. He does this in anticipation of reaping a fall harvest.

> *This is why expecting to receive what God promised is so important. If you don't expect anything, you won't receive anything.*

Talking of his work among them, the Apostle Paul said to the Corinthian church, *"He who plows should plow in hope, and he who threshes in hope should be partaker of his hope"* (1 Cor. 9:10).

The word hope carries with it the idea of expecting. The *New Living Translation* of this verse makes this very clear: *"The one who plows and the one who threshes the grain might both EXPECT a share of the harvest."*

Charles Spurgeon once said, "You might not always get what you want, but you always get what you expect."[2]

This is why expecting to receive what God promised is so important. If you don't expect anything, you won't receive anything. God watches over His Word to perform it. But His hands are tied until someone in faith *expects* to receive.

Three Attitudes

Basically, there are three levels of expectation. You'll find that people generally fall into one of these three categories.

First, some people don't expect anything. They do this so they are guaranteed never to be disappointed.

Second, there are those who do expect something but never receive anything. They're often frustrated and wonder why they never get what they need. Then they often blame God for their lack of receiving.

Third, there are people who expect to receive, and they receive what they expect. Life always seems to go their way, and others often wonder why. The reason is found in their attitude toward the Word of God.

How Valuable Is the Word to You?

The way we esteem Scripture determines the level of our expectation. Look at what Paul wrote regarding this: *"For this reason we also thank God without ceasing, because when you received the word of God which you heard from us, you welcomed it not as the word of men, but as it is in truth, the word of God, which also effectively works in you who believe"* (1 Thess. 2:13).

Paul commended the Thessalonians because when they heard the Word, they recognized and received it as God's Word.

To receive what God has for you, you must do the same. You have to accept Scripture as God speaking directly to you. Some people, however, don't recognize the Bible as the inspired Word of God.

Similar But Not the Same

Two cars with the same exterior color and interior styling parked side by side can look identical. However, one has a bigger engine, so it's much faster. On the surface, the cars look the same. But one can win races while the other is simply driven to and from work.

Some people look at the Bible like this. They think it's just like any other book. But it's very different!

The writer of Hebrews called the Bible alive and powerful—a sword that divides the soul and spirit (Heb. 4:12).

> To receive what God has for you, . . . you have to accept Scripture as God speaking directly to you.

9

The Apostle John considered the words of Jesus Spirit-breathed and spiritual life to those who believe (John 6:63). And the Apostle Peter said the Bible is the incorruptible, indestructible, ever-powerful, eternal Word of God (1 Peter 1:23).

When my dad was a teenager, he wrote in the flyleaf of his Bible, "God said it. I believe it. And that settles it." He said this often, and so do I. My dad believed and I believe that the Word of God is infallible. If we don't look at the Bible like this, the promises contained in it will have little impact on our lives.

Is the Word of God your everything? It is to me. I expect God to take care of me. It doesn't matter what's going on in the economy. It makes no difference what is happening in the government or what laws have been changed. It doesn't matter what kind of extreme weather is battering our nation or what disease is trying to come on our bodies. The Bible is filled with promises we can stand on in any situation.

> God said it.
> I believe it.
> And that settles it.
> —Kenneth E. Hagin

Expectant Faith

Mark chapter 11 records the story of Jesus cursing the fig tree. He and His disciples were walking to Jerusalem when Jesus saw a fig tree in the distance. He was hungry, so He went to the tree to get some fruit.

When Jesus and the disciples reached the tree, they couldn't find any figs. Jesus said to the tree, *"Let no one eat fruit from you ever again"* (Mark 11:14). His disciples heard Him say that.

The next day when they passed by the same spot, Peter said, *"Rabbi, look! The fig tree which You cursed has withered away"* (v. 21). You can tell by his response that when he heard Jesus speak to the tree, he never expected anything to happen.

If Peter really believed that Jesus' words would come to pass, he wouldn't have been surprised to see a dead tree. J.M. Farro said, "If we pray, but don't really expect God to answer us, we shouldn't be surprised if He doesn't."[3]

> *If we pray, but don't really expect God to answer us, we shouldn't be surprised if He doesn't.*
> —J.M. Farro

For our faith to work, we have to believe that God will do what He said. We're either expecting or we're not. When we say, "I believe that will happen," we're actually saying, "I expect that to happen."

An example of expectant faith is found in Acts chapter 27 when the ship Paul was in was about to be wrecked by a storm on the island of Malta. Paul was being taken as a prisoner to Rome to stand trial before Caesar. When the ship first set sail, the weather was good. Before long, however, a storm arose. The crew battled the tempest for so long that Scripture says they *"gave up all hope of being saved"* (Acts 27:20 NIV).

The passengers and crew on this ship did not believe they would make it through the storm. They expected to die. But Paul stood before them and said:

ACTS 27:22–25 (NIV)
22 "But now I urge you to keep up your courage, because not one of you will be lost; only the ship will be destroyed.

23 Last night an angel of the God to whom I belong and whom I serve stood beside me

24 and said, 'Do not be afraid, Paul. You must stand trial before Caesar; and God has graciously given you the lives of all who sail with you.'

25 So keep up your courage, men, for I have faith in God that it will happen just as he told me."

One Word Makes a Big Difference

Hearing one word from God can and will change our expectation level. We can go from no expectation to great expectation in less than 60 seconds!

At one time Paul thought their outcome would be different. He said in verse 10 (NIV), *"Men, I can see that our voyage is going to be disastrous and bring great loss to ship and cargo, and to our own lives also."*

However, the word of the angel caused Paul to go from despair to expectation. When he told the men on the ship what the angel said, their expectation changed too.

One word can help us make it through every storm. We can expect victory instead of defeat. We can expect God to answer our prayers and fulfill His promises.

What are you expecting?

Scriptures to Ponder

PROVERBS 23:18 (AMP)

18 Surely there is a future [and a reward], and your hope and expectation will not be cut off.

PROVERBS 24:14 (NIV)

14 Know also that wisdom is like honey for you: If you find it, there is a future hope for you, and your hope will not be cut off.

1 PETER 1:3

3 Blessed be the God and Father of our Lord Jesus Christ, who according to His abundant mercy has begotten us again to a living hope through the resurrection of Jesus Christ from the dead.

Power Points

Expectation is a driving force behind your faith. Without it, you will never see your dreams come to pass. The key to pressing through hard times is staying built up in the Word. One word from God can turn around any situation.

Just Sayin'

Proclaim Your Victory!

- God said it. I believe it. That settles it. I will take the limits off of my thinking and expect God to do what He said. Nothing, absolutely nothing, is impossible for Him.

- I will not be defeated. I will stand firm until I see what I am believing God for come to pass.

Action Items

1. What are you expecting? List three things.

   a._____

   b._____

   c._____

2. What scriptures are you standing on? Write down at least one scripture for each of the three items you listed above.

   a._____

   b._____

   c._____

3. What do you feel are your biggest hindrances to receiving the three things you listed?

_____

_____

_____

4. What can you do to overcome these hindrances?

_____

_____

_____

---

[1]brainyquote.com/quotes/quotes/e/earlnighti379870.html
[2]brainyquote.com/quotes/quotes/c/charlesspu130021.html
[3]jesusfreakhideout.com/devotionals/act.asp

2
Nothing Is Too Big for God

Have you ever felt like you're caught in a river of circumstance? You've tried to get out of the boat, but the current is swift and the water is rough. It doesn't look like there's any escape.

King David's life was like that. The Book of Psalms is filled with passages about times when he cried out to God. The anguish and difficulties he went through are clear.

One thing that stands out about David is how he reacted to adversity. Regardless of what came against him, he always kept his eyes on God. David *always* expected God to help him.

Expectation is an attitude to embrace. We need it to get through adversity, but we also need it when we're standing in faith to receive something from God. Lamentations 3:25 (AMPC) says, *"The Lord is good to those who wait hopefully and EXPECTANTLY for Him."*

Time and again, David cried out, "God, I'm expecting You to help me!" He never doubted God's love and faithfulness.

How could David be so confident? God was the rock David stood on. To him God's Word was everything, and he highly esteemed it. He said, *"That is why I wait expectantly, trusting God to help, for he has promised"* (Ps. 130:5 TLB).

God was David's salvation, defense, glory, strength, and refuge. We can see this clearly in the following verses.

PSALM 62:5–7

5 My soul, wait silently for God alone, for my expectation is from Him.

6 He only is my rock and my salvation; He is my defense; I shall not be moved.

7 In God is my salvation and my glory; the rock of my strength, and my refuge, is in God.

A Trusted Word

Has someone ever assured you that he would help you? Maybe you were moving and he promised to help pack boxes and load the truck.

Because of your relationship, you knew you could trust his word. It never crossed your mind that he wouldn't show up.

> God doesn't have favorites. What He did for David, He'll do for us if we'll look to Him.

We need to extend that same trust to God. Yet this is often not the case. It's strange that some people can trust other people easier than they can trust God. Why is it so hard to believe that God will do what He said?

The writer of Psalm 71 said that God had been his confidence since his youth (v. 5 NIV). As a young shepherd boy, David relied on God for protection and help when he fought the lion and the bear. That reliance never changed throughout David's life. No matter what difficulty he encountered, God never let him down one time. David knew God would always be there.

The same is true for us. God doesn't have favorites (Acts 10:34). What He *did* for David, He'll *do* for us if we'll look to Him.

The Hazards of Doubt and Unbelief

Have you ever noticed that life has an ebb and flow to it? In some seasons we're on a mountaintop. At other times it seems as if all kinds of stuff is piled on top of us. The question we must ask is, "What do we do when trouble comes our way?"

Doubt limits what God can do for us. Nothing is hopeless or impossible to Him, but our unbelief stops His hand. Charles L. Allen said, "When you say a situation or a person is hopeless, you are slamming the door in the face of God."[1]

No matter the circumstances, nothing is too big for God. When we realize this and take God at His Word, our lives will be so much better.

> However many blessings we expect from God, His infinite liberality will always exceed all our wishes and thoughts.
> —John Calvin

John Calvin made this statement: "However many blessings we expect from God, His infinite liberality will always exceed all our wishes and thoughts."[2] If we'll keep our confidence in God, He will do far more than we ever thought possible (Eph. 3:20)!

Don't Waver, Wane, or Wonder

When people pray and nothing happens, they wonder why. While there could be many reasons, here are two prevalent ones.

First, James, the brother of Jesus, tells us that our prayers need to be faith-filled (James 1:6). But how many times have we brought a request to the Lord and when nothing happened by the following week, we began to wonder?

> If God said it, you can expect it!

During times like this, it's best to follow David's advice. He said, *"In the morning I lay my requests before you and WAIT expectantly"* (Ps. 5:3 NIV). He didn't put a time limit on his prayers. He stayed in faith until he saw his answer.

When our expectation wanes and we wonder if God will come through, James says that our loyalty is divided (James 1:6–7 NLT). Because we're double-minded, we're not in faith. The end result is that we won't receive anything from the Lord.

Quit Thinking!

A second reason people don't receive answers to their prayers is that they can't see the result. Instead of simply trusting Him, they try to figure it out. They think, "How in the world is this going to work out?"

The answer to that question is—it doesn't matter. If God said it, you can expect it! You will never be able to figure out how God will do something. But if you'll believe what He says and not let your words be different from His Word, you'll find that you'll start receiving what you've asked for.

How to Hang In There

Although the time between praying and receiving can seem long, staying focused on the promises of God will help you not to become discouraged. Plunging into God's promises will keep you focused on what He can do.

When some people go swimming, they first put their toes in the water. They want to test it to see how cold it is. Personally, I think it's better just to jump in! The water will be the same temperature whether you put your toes in or dive in!

People do the same thing with the promises of God. They poke around the edges. But if you really want to receive what God has for you, then you have to jump in.

Do Great Things for God

What would you do if you knew that God was always ready to help you? Would you try to do more than you're doing right now? Would you try to do what you have always dreamed of doing? Would you dare to attempt what others say is impossible?

The reason men and women attempt great things for God is that they believe He will act on their behalf. When things aren't going well, their faith and hope are still in the Lord. With the psalmist, they say, *"O my soul, don't be discouraged. Don't be upset. Expect God to act! For I know that I shall again have plenty of reason to praise him for all that he will do. He is my help! He is my God!"* (Ps. 42:11 TLB).

> *The reason men and women attempt great things for God is that they believe He will act on their behalf.*

We can anticipate that God will show up when our faith is placed solidly in His Word and when we declare, "I expect it to be as You said."

I like what William Carey, known as the father of modern missions, said: "Expect great things from God. Attempt great things for God."[3] In an atmosphere of expectation, God's mighty power shows up and manifests itself.

The degree of your expectation often determines the degree of power that is manifested. If you think nothing much will happen, nothing much will. But if you're expecting a lot, then great things will take place. Charles F. Kettering, the inventor of the electric starter, said, "High achievement always takes place in the framework of high expectations."[4]

Expectation is simply believing that you can. Every time I competed in a sporting event, I expected to win. If you don't have this kind of attitude, you'll never win. That's because you won't give it all you've got. You won't put everything you have into the game.

God's Ready—Are You?

What has God called you to do? Not everyone is called to full-time ministry. God's plan for some is to work in secular business or in some other field. Wherever you are, you are called to make an impact. What are you expecting God to do for you and through you?

> Expectant faith is the trigger that causes God to move.

God is always there ready to help. The Holy Spirit is waiting to move on your behalf when you trust Him. The Holy Spirit is the power of God moving in your life. Expectant faith is the trigger that causes God to move.

Don't ever think that God will do less than what He said in His Word. If He said it, He'll do it. If God spoke it, He'll bring it to pass!

This is the hour to expect a great God to do great things. This is the time to step out and do great things with Him and for Him. He will meet you at your level of expectation and do what He has promised in His Word.

Scriptures to Ponder

LAMENTATIONS 3:25 (AMPC)
25 The Lord is good to those who wait hopefully and expectantly for Him.

PSALM 130:5 (NLT)
5 I am counting on the Lord; yes, I am counting on him. I have put my hope in his word.

EPHESIANS 3:20 (NLT)
20 Now all glory to God, who is able, through his mighty power at work within us, to accomplish infinitely more than we might ask or think.

Power Points

God is not only with us—He is also in us. Because of this, we can boldly step out and do great things in life, whether we're called to the ministry or to some other work. God will lead and guide us each step of the way so our lives make a huge impact.

Just Sayin'

Proclaim Your Victory!

- God is my rock and defense. I shall not be moved.
- God is for me and not against me. He is in me, and He will never leave me nor forsake me. Therefore, I will push harder, go further, and do more because I know God will move on my behalf.

Action Items

1. How do you react to adversity?

   _____

   _____

   _____

2. List three "go-to" scriptures you can stand on when adversity strikes.

   a._____

   b._____

   c._____

3. What can you do to overcome doubt?

   _____

   _____

   _____

4. What is the first step you can take to achieve or receive what you are expecting from God?

   _____

   _____

   _____

5. If you haven't taken that first step, what is holding you back?

   _____

   _____

   _____

---

[1]brainyquote.com/quotes/quotes/c/charlesla105860.html
[2]brainyquote.com/quotes/quotes/j/johncalvin182884.html
[3]goodreads.com/quotes/154702-expect-great-things-from-god-attempt-great-things-for-god
[4]brainyquote.com/quotes/authors/c/charles_kettering.html

3
Everything Is Subject to Change

Everyone would agree—Job went through a rough period in his life. He was a man of great wealth but had a sudden turn of devastating events. He wound up in a dire situation.

In a very short time, Job lost almost all of his earthly possessions. All of his children died when the house where they were eating collapsed on them. Then Job became severely afflicted with painful boils that covered his body.

At times like this, you hope those closest to you will offer comforting words of support. This didn't happen for Job. His wife told him to curse God and die. Job's "good" friends accused him of living in sin. They reasoned that his misfortune had to be of his own doing and God was punishing him.

Use your imagination for a moment and see Job sitting in an ash heap discussing his situation with his friends. In the midst of despair, he desperately strained to see a ray of hope. Gazing toward the distant horizon, he said, *"When a man dies, will he come back to life? If so, I would wait all the days of my struggle until my relief comes"* (Job 14:14 HCSB).

Don't Listen to Satan's Lies

Job's situation is not unlike that of some people today. Many are caught in the grip of quiet despair. They have resigned themselves to believing that their lives will never get any better. They go through their daily routines with no hope for change. They've sunk into depression and can't imagine a better tomorrow.

These men and women no longer look toward the horizon of possibility. Instead, they keep walking on the treadmill of unchanging circumstances. They've accepted Satan's lie that nothing will ever change for them.

Your Circumstances Are Temporary

Job realized that what he was going through was temporary. And he was determined to wait until his circumstances turned around.

From the beginning of time, God ordained a normal process of change. Genesis 8:22 says, *"While the earth remains, seed-time and harvest, cold and heat, winter and summer, and day and night shall not cease."* Things on the earth are designed to change. If something doesn't, it's abnormal.

For example, if it's hot outside, we know the temperature won't stay that way forever. The temperature in Oklahoma fluctuates so much that we often say, "If you don't like the weather, just wait. It will soon change!"

Over the course of time, change happens naturally. Things wear out. People get older. Some people don't have as much hair as they once did. And for many, their hair has turned gray!

> Things on the earth are designed to change. If something doesn't, it's abnormal.

On a positive note, life can get better. You can get a better job making more money. Some people move into a new home or buy a new car. Others fall in love and get married.

Hopeful for a Better Day

Mankind is wired to hope for better things. God made us that way. We hope that our future will be better than our past.

Our hope is challenged when things don't get better. If we're sick, we want to get well. When we don't have enough money, it's natural to start looking for ways to bring in more income. But if we don't get better or can't find a new job, our hope can begin to fade.

During times like this, we have to realize that whatever we are going through is temporary. Our circumstances are not always going to be this way. *Everything* is subject to change. When the Apostle Paul was going through troubles, he called them a *"light affliction, which is but for a moment"* (2 Cor. 4:17).

> Mankind is wired to hope for better things.

Start Talking

If you don't like where you are or what is happening in your life, take possession of your future with your mouth. What you're facing may look like a mountain, but Jesus told us in Mark 11:23 that we can speak to mountains, and they will move.

Don't be silent about what you want to see. This is an area where some Christians miss it. They believe the Word, but they're not seeing anything happen. Often it's because they're not saying anything. Let your confession continually be, "Change is on the way. My circumstances will not stay the same." As I've often preached, "Keep saying it until you see it."

25

If your life is going pretty well, know that there's more. You can go to a higher level. God never wants you to reach a certain point and stop. He wants you to continually move forward.

Wait . . . Patiently

Job had to be patient and hold on to his hope for a better tomorrow. Patience helped him persevere until change came. Waiting is never anyone's favorite thing to do, especially today. We've become a society that wants everything now. No one wants to wait for anything anymore.

Notice again what Job said: *"I will wait, till my change comes"* (Job 14:14). The meaning of the Hebrew word translated *wait* implies being *patient* and *hopeful*. Job was patiently looking forward to a better time.

> When patience is fully developed, it will keep us from quitting.

Patience never resigns itself to a situation without expecting change. It confidently waits, knowing that it will possess what it expects.

James, the brother of Jesus, tells us to count it all joy when we fall into various trials. That's because trials cause our faith to be tested and allow our patience to grow. When patience is fully developed, it will keep us from quitting. As a result, we won't lack any of the things we are believing God for (James 1:2–4).

Romans 5:5 says, "Now hope does not disappoint, because the love of God has been poured out in our hearts by the Holy Spirit who was given to us." We've been given the mighty Holy Spirit Who is working in our lives. We won't be disappointed if we will stand still and wait on Him to move in our situations.

Stuff's Going On . . . Behind the Scenes

Just because we can't see anything happening doesn't mean that God is not working. He's working behind the scenes. He often has to rearrange some things in the spirit realm before we see anything change in our lives.

God wants to reveal His glory in the midst of your trial. When it's all said and done, you'll be like the Apostle Paul who said, "I always triumph in Christ" (2 Cor. 2:14).

> God wants to reveal His glory in the midst of your trial.

Sometimes God has to work on the inside of you so you can receive what you need. For instance, unforgiveness will rob you of His blessings. Some people hold on to everything. Once I forgive someone, I forget about it. If you're not like this, you may need to make some adjustments on the inside. When you do, God can move on your behalf. There will never be permanent change on the outside (in your situation) until change first takes place on the inside (in your heart).

The Master of Change

God's Word is forever settled in Heaven (Ps. 119:89), and He never changes (Mal. 3:6). Scripture says that Jesus is *"the same yesterday, today, and forever"* (Heb. 13:8).

Our Heavenly Father is an unchanging God Who reigns over this constantly changing world. We can say that He is the master of change. He brings supernatural change to the natural world.

27

God makes the impossible possible and the invisible visible. He can do the unthinkable and achieve the incredible. Nothing is too hard for Him! Nothing can overcome Him or take His place!

It's through God's unchanging promises that we can live the good life He has for us. If we want to experience what God promised in Scripture, we have to be willing to line our lives up with His Word. Some Christians are unwilling to do this, so they never enjoy all of His blessings.

Some people get just inside the door of salvation and stop there. But there's a whole lot more to salvation than escaping the flames of hell. So keep moving forward in your walk with the Lord. You can never exhaust the depths of His goodness.

Tap Into the Blood of Jesus!

God sent Jesus to the cross so our lives could be better. The blood that He shed at Calvary has never lost its power!

> The blood of Christ changes us from sinners to saints, from something vile to something worthwhile.

The blood of Christ changes us from sinners to saints, from something vile to something worthwhile. Because of the blood, we can go from being on the outside looking in to being on the inside looking out. We can go from being rejected to being accepted.

When old-time prayer warriors were up against a situation that needed to be changed, they would cry out, "I plead the blood!" They knew that the power in the blood of Jesus could change any situation.

Tap Into the Change Maker!

The Holy Spirit has been given to us and lives in us. He is greater, stronger, bigger, mightier, and more powerful than anything we will ever face! He will help us in every situation. We may get in a panic, but He never does. To us, our situation may look impossible. But to God, it's possible.

When we get a hold of Jesus and the Word and recognize that the Holy Spirit lives in us, our lives will never be the same. Our minds can be renewed. Our bodies can be healed. Our families can be restored. Our circumstances can change!

When it seems like all is lost, don't give up. God says, "I can change that." When everything looks like it's over, your Heavenly Father says, "It's not over. I'm changing it."

It's easy to look at your situation and give in to the pressure that surrounds you. But in the middle of your circumstances, start expecting them to change. In the middle of the biggest mess you've ever been in, say, "Something good is going to happen to me!" No matter what is going on, you can believe God's Word, speak it, and expect it to come to pass in your life.

As you relax and wait patiently on the Lord, your change, like Job's, will come. Hold on tightly to God's promises. Let His power and ability work on your behalf. You will see what everyone said could never happen—happen!

Scriptures to Ponder

ROMANS 5:5 (NLT)

5   And this hope will not lead to disappointment. For we know how dearly God loves us, because he has given us the Holy Spirit to fill our hearts with his love.

2 CORINTHIANS 2:14

14 Now thanks be to God who always leads us in triumph in Christ, and through us diffuses the fragrance of His knowledge in every place.

Power Points

No matter how long you've been in a seemingly impossible situation, know that it is subject to change. There is hope for a better day. At times like this, put a guard on your mouth. Don't give voice to how things are, but continually talk about what you want to see. When you do this, it won't be long before you'll have what you're saying.

Just Sayin'

Proclaim Your Victory!

- I look to the horizon of possibility and expect God's best in my life. No matter where I am in the Lord, my life will get better.

- Change is coming. My circumstances will not stay this way. Something good is about to happen to me.

Action Items

1. In what area is your hope challenged? What can you do to change this?

_____

_____

_____

2. What are you saying about your situation? Pay attention to your words. Write down three things that you constantly confess about what you expect.

a._____

b._____

c._____

3. Do you need to change your confession?

_____

_____

_____

4. If so, write down a positive confession to counter each negative confession you have been making.

_____

_____

_____

4
Did You Ask?

Life is a series of expectations. You're expecting something either good or bad. Some people are pessimistic and are always sure the worst will happen. Others are optimistic and look for the best, no matter what is going on around them.

Our expectations are based on words. If somebody said, "Hold out your hand. I have something for you," you probably would immediately reach out an eager hand.

Parents have said to their kids, "If you get all of the yard work done, we'll do such-and-such." The children then look forward to what they've been promised.

The same is true when you're told you're getting a raise. As soon as you receive your paycheck, you look to make sure the extra money is there! Some people have even bought something new *before* they saw the raise. They did this because they believed what their supervisor told them. Before they saw an increase, they acted like they already had it.

God Is a Good Father

Based on what God promised in Scripture, we can expect good things. We can also be sure that He is always ready, willing, and able to pour out His blessings on us.

Most earthly fathers help their kids and grandchildren all they can. I have five grandsons, and if they want something, they call Poppy.

"Poppy, I need new cleats." "Poppy, I need a new bat." "Poppy, I need new shoulder pads and a new helmet."

You know what Poppy says? "OK." Why? I love those boys. If it's within my power, I am going to make it happen for them.

Your Heavenly Father is the same way. It's sad to say, but some fathers don't help their kids. God is not like that. He wants to help His children more than any earthly father does. Scripture says, *"As bad as you are, you still know how to give good gifts to your children. But your heavenly Father is even more ready to give good things to people who ask"* (Matt. 7:11 CEV).

> [God] wants to help His children more than any earthly father does.

Willing and Able

If you need something, you probably won't ask a stranger. You'll talk to someone you have a relationship with, because you're pretty sure that person will listen to you. A stranger can just walk on by.

If someone told you he'd like to give you $20,000, you'd want to believe him. However, his word is only as good as his resources and his willingness to do what he has said. If you don't know whether he is *able* to give you the money, you may not put much stock in his offer.

Another person may say he wants to give you $20,000. You know he has the resources, but you also know he's not always willing to let go of them. You're still not sure if you'll ever see the money.

34

The good news is that God has *both* the resources *and* the willingness to help you. All you have to do is ask for what He has promised you in the Bible.

It's Up to You

In his book *How to Enjoy Plenty*, T.L. Osborne wrote, "When the mind perceives God's abundance and begins to comprehend that He created the wealth of this earth for the blessings of His children, the walls of mental enslavement begin to crumble and the rainbow of God's plenty appears"[1]

A big problem for a lot of Christians is that they are trapped by their circumstances and see no way out. They are saved and filled with the Spirit, but they haven't taken the time to read the Word. Although they know that God promised them something, they're really not sure what He said He would do.

> Heaven must be full of answers for which no one has ever bothered to ask.
> —Cameron Thompson

These Christians lack the knowledge of God's Word that will give them hope for a better future. They really don't know how willing God is to help them. So they try to get through the situation on their own.

You Have to Ask

Notice the last part of Matthew 7:11. It says that God will give good things to *"people who ask."* Matthew makes it clear that we have to ask. Cameron Thompson said, "Heaven must be full of answers for which no one has ever bothered to ask."[2] That is a powerful statement!

If you're in a store and see something in a locked case, you have to ask the sales associate to get it for you in order to hold it and look at it closely. You can stand by the case all day. You can dream about the item and tell others how nice it is and how much you want it. But until you ask the sales associate to see it, it's staying in the locked case.

I preach about the promises of God all the time. But until I personally ask God for what He has promised, I'm not going to get anything.

One time many years ago, I was making plans to go to a baseball game with some guys I worked with. One of the men really wanted to go but didn't have the money. Someone in the group preached a mini sermon to him on believing God for finances.

When it came time to collect the money for the tickets, the guy who preached the mini sermon didn't have it. It was only a few days earlier that he preached to his friend, but he ended up not having the money!

This is an example of how you can know all about something but not get it yourself! Until you open your mouth and ask God for what you want or need, you're not getting anything.

It's Time to Grow Up

I have had people say to me, "I just can't understand why so-and-so is always getting stuff!"

In talking to them, I learned that they've never prayed and asked God to meet their need. They thought that God knew what they needed, so they never bothered going to Him concerning their situation.

Some people think God is moved by our need. He's not. He's not moved by our emotions or tears either. What moves God to perform His Word? Faith.

Other people have said, "I don't understand. I've been saved longer than that person. Look what they're getting from God."

It doesn't matter how long you've been saved. A person can be saved for 24 hours, ask God for something, and receive it. Someone else can be saved for 24 years. But if he never asks God in faith, he's not going to get what he needs.

When your children are young, you'll get them something to drink when they ask. But when they get older, you expect them to get their own water when they're thirsty. If your 12-year-old asks for a drink, you'll probably tell him to get it himself!

In the same way God expects His children to grow up. When you are first born again, it seems like it's easy to get healed or receive any of the promises of God. It's like being a kid in a candy store!

After awhile, it doesn't seem so easy. You may not have realized it, but others have carried you. It was really their faith, not yours, that got the results. Now God expects you to get in the Word and ask Him for what belongs to you.

When Dad Prayed and Nothing Happened!

When I was 15 years old, I got an infection in my left ear. It hurt so bad I could hardly stand it. Dad was in California at the time, so I called him. I expected him to pray and I would be fine. That's what I had done all my life. This time when Dad prayed, nothing happened! It was the first time Dad's prayers for me hadn't worked!

I went to my pastor, Brother Leonard Wood, and asked him to pray. There was nothing wrong with the way he prayed. But again, nothing happened.

EXPECT

Since my ear wasn't any better, I went to the doctor. He said the infection was caused by a fungus that lives in damp climates. Soldiers who had served in the South Sea Islands during World War II brought it to the States.

At that time we were living in Port Arthur, Texas, which is on the coast. The main street of Port Arthur is right at sea level. In fact, in the junior high school I attended, you had to go to the second floor before you could see over the dike.

The humidity is really high in Port Arthur. Sometimes when I lay down at night, the sheets were so damp that it felt like someone had poured water on them!

The doctor said the fungus was incurable, but it could be controlled. He told us if we moved to the desert of California or Arizona, it would help.

The doctor went on to say that I should never swim again. And he added that I needed to be really careful never to get any water in that ear. He gave me chartreuse-colored ear drops. I'd put them in my ear and then stuff in a piece of cotton.

When Dad came home, I told him I needed to go the doctor to get my ear cleaned out. He took me and stayed in the car while I ran into the doctor's office.

When I got back in the car Dad asked, "Do you want to get healed?"

"You know I do."

Dad didn't say anything else. He just sat there.

"Are you going to tell me?" I finally asked.

"I was waiting on you to ask," he replied. "Son," he continued. "If you're going to get your healing, you're going to have to believe for yourself. I was praying about this, and the Lord showed me that you know as much about faith as anybody."

This was true. I had even preached some of Dad's sermons to the youth in our church. It suddenly hit me like a rock. I'm preaching to others, yet I'm expecting my dad to carry me.

> *You can go to your Heavenly Father the same way you do your earthly father. You can ask God for what the Bible says belongs to you.*

When we got back to the house, Dad pointed to a chair and said, "Let's kneel down here and pray."

I knelt by the chair and Dad knelt by the couch. I waited and finally asked, "Are you going to pray?"

"No. I don't need anything."

I prayed, and from that moment on I began quoting the Word and thanking God for my healing. The manifestation didn't come immediately, but within two weeks all of the pain was gone. My ear was healed!

In 1962 when I went into the Army, I had to have a hearing test. The doctors said that my left ear was a lot stronger than my right ear.

This is where a lot of people in faith circles are today. They've heard about faith from many different preachers and teachers. But they're not receiving from God. They have faith in their heart, but they're not putting it into action. They want others to pray and believe that God will do something for them. They don't understand that they can pray and God will hear them.

You can go to your Heavenly Father the same way you do your earthly father. You can ask God for what the Bible says belongs to you. Here are six practical ways to increase your faith and raise your expectation level so you can receive what is already yours.

Number One—Maintain a Diet of God's Word

Meditate on scriptures that talk about the goodness of God. Think on Bible verses that tell you who you are in Christ.

Remind yourself of scripture that covers what you are asking for. My dad always used to tell people to find scriptures that promised them the things they were praying for.

As you meditate on these scriptures, you're building your faith, and you'll have a solid foundation to stand on.

Number Two—Pray in the Spirit

Spend time praying in tongues. The Holy Spirit will tell you things to do that will help you receive from Him.

> Praying in tongues will help you be more sensitive to what God wants you to do.

Many people are more body conscious than they are spirit conscious. When situations arise, they are ruled by what they see, feel, and hear rather than being led by the Spirit. Others are more mental and intellectual. Everything has to be reasoned out and logically correct for them. Our feelings and intellect, however, are not enough for us to successfully follow God.

Praying in tongues will help you be more sensitive to what God wants you to do. The more you pray in tongues, the more the voices of your body, emotions, and intellect will grow dim. You'll learn to recognize the voice of the inward witness of the Spirit more easily.

One way to describe the inward witness is that you have an inner peace. As you learn to follow that peace, it will be a governing factor in your life.

Number Three—Hang Around Encouragers

You cannot hang around people who are filled with doubt and unbelief and have your faith work. They will pull you down. You may not think so, but they will.

Most people have secular jobs, and worldly things may be going on in the workplace all the time. This is why the Bible tells us not to forsake the assembling of ourselves together (Heb. 10:25). When we go to church, we're strengthened and encouraged by the minister's sermon and by our brothers and sisters in the Lord.

George M. Adams said, "Encouragement is oxygen to the soul."[3] Isn't it refreshing when somebody gives you a word of encouragement in the middle of difficulty? We all need people to encourage us, and we also need to encourage others.

Number Four—Remember What God Did

It's good to remember what God has already done for us. Remember how He helped you, provided for you, healed you, and protected you. If He did it once, He'll do it again. Relive the times when God helped you accomplish something that everybody said was impossible. It will help build your faith.

Number Five—Read the Stories of Others

The Bible is filled with stories of how God helped people. Shadrach, Meshach, and Abednego; Abraham, Isaac, and Jacob; Paul, Peter, and many more. If He helped all of these people, He will help you too.

Seeing how they persevered will help you remain steadfast and stand strong until you receive. The inspiration you'll get from reading these Bible stories will help build up your faith and expectation.

Number Six—Get in a Corporate Atmosphere of Faith

God doesn't want any of His children to stand alone. We are part of the Body of Christ. And we're supposed to support and lift up each other.

Many times the enemy causes people to turn away from the church instead of turning to it. Anytime you are experiencing challenges, church is where you need to be.

There is a corporate atmosphere of faith in a body of believers. You may come to church feeling down and caught up in your situation. But when you come together with your brothers and sisters in the Lord, your faith is joined with theirs. Instead of wondering how you're going to make it, you are encouraged and your faith is strengthened.

If you'll lift your eyes toward God in faith instead of focusing on your circumstances, you'll begin to see what He has for you. Then you can confidently ask Him for the things you need and receive what you ask for.

Scriptures to Ponder

PHILIPPIANS 4:6 (AMP)

6   Do not be anxious *or* worried about anything, but in everything [every circumstance and situation] by prayer and petition with thanksgiving, continue to make your [specific] requests known to God.

PSALM 107:6 (NIV)

6   Then they cried out to the Lord in their trouble, and he deliv-
     ered them from their distress.

JOHN 16:24

24   Until now you have asked nothing in My name. Ask, and you
     will receive, that your joy may be full.

Power Points

God is a loving Heavenly Father. He hears and answers the
prayers of His children. He doesn't have favorites or listen to one
of His children more than others. We all have equal access to His
throne. We can confidently and boldly ask Him for anything in line
with His Word and expect Him to move on our behalf.

Just Sayin'

Proclaim Your Victory!

- Whether my need is big or little, God is ready, willing, and
  able to pour out His blessings on me.

- I am sensitive to the leading of the Holy Spirit. I'll go where
  He directs. And when He prompts me not to go somewhere
  or do something, I will stay put.

- I purpose to be a person who encourages others.

Action Items

1. What is the biggest thing you think God can do for you?

---

2. What is the biggest thing you think God can do for you right now.

_____

_____

_____

3. How has God come through for you in the past? Write down three things He has done. Review this list every day for the next month.

a. _____

b. _____

c. _____

4. Are you an optimist or a pessimist?_____
Gratitude shifts a negative mindset to a positive one.
Every day for the next 21 days, write down what you are grateful for. (Record your comments in the Gratitude Journal, starting on page 67.)

5. What is your favorite Bible story of how God provided for, delivered, or healed someone? _____

_____

Read this story every day for the next month.

6. Who can agree with you in prayer concerning what you are believing for? _____

_____

If you need someone to agree with you in prayer, call our prayer line at (918) 258-1588, ext. 5566. The phones are answered Monday through Friday from 8:15 a.m. to 4:30 p.m. (CST). One of our prayer partners will pray with you.

If you prefer, you may email us at partnerservice@rhema.org or write us at:

Kenneth Hagin Ministries
P.O. Box 50126
Tulsa, OK 74150-0126

---

[1]Osborn, T.L. *How To Enjoy Plenty* (Tulsa, Oklahoma. OSFO Int'l. 1977), 16.
[2]As quoted by Ruth Bell Graham in *Legacy of a Pack Rat* (Nashville, Tennessee. Oliver-Nelson Books, 1989), 151.
[3]spiritual-quotes-to-live-by.com/soul-quotes.html.

5
Finishing What Was Started

When Lynette and I started in ministry, I was an evangelist. In 1966 if you were going to get any meetings, your wife had to play the piano and sing. It helped if you could sing too.

Believe it or not, Lynette and I sang a few duets together. We had about three songs we sang. Lynette's singing is great. Mine? Well, let's just say that I sing in the cracks between the notes! If I'm standing beside somebody who's pretty good, I can usually slide to where that person is.

Lynette used to sing the hymn "We've Come This Far by Faith" by Albert A. Goodson. I like the line that goes, "He's never failed me yet." When you think about it, compared with God and what He can and will do, everything else is small stuff.

The devil often screams in our ears that God won't come through. When he says this, we have to just hold on to our Heavenly Father and not let go. This is when we have to remember how big God is. He's greater than any problem we will ever face.

During times like that, instead of worrying about our circumstances, we need to focus on God's faithfulness. Instead of pondering our problems, we must press into His promises. One of those promises is found in the Book of Philippians.

PHILIPPIANS 1:6 (AMPC)

6 And I am convinced and sure of this very thing, that He Who BEGAN a good work in you will CONTINUE until the day of Jesus Christ [right up to the time of His return], developing [that good work] and perfecting and BRINGING IT TO FULL COMPLETION in you.

In this verse, Paul is expressing his complete confidence in God. The commentary *Barnes' Notes on the New Testament* states that being confident means "to be fully and firmly persuaded or convinced . . . Paul was *entirely convinced* of the truth of what he said. It is the language of a man who had no doubt on the subject."[1]

Paul mentioned three things in this verse that he believed God would do for the Philippian believers. I believe God wants to do these same things in your life too. First, God *began* a good work. Second, He will *continue* that work. And third, God will *finish* what He started.

Number One—God Began a Good Work in You

In Acts chapter 3 we read the story of the healing of a lame man at the temple gate called Beautiful. This crippled man was begging for money when Peter and John were walking into the temple to pray.

Peter noticed the man and said, "Look at us." The man looked up, expecting to get something. Other people were walking by, but he gave his attention to the disciples.

> Being confident means "to be fully and firmly persuaded or convinced."

The lame man may have been disappointed for a moment when Peter said, "I don't have any money." The crippled man had to make a decision. Should he continue looking at Peter and John? Or should he try to get money from others?

Peter continued, "What I have, I am going to give you. In the Name of Jesus Christ of Nazareth, rise and walk!"

Although this man had been crippled from birth, he received something worth far more than any amount of money. He was healed! He could walk!

The man went with Peter and John into the temple. He leaped and walked up and down Solomon's porch! Everyone there knew this was the beggar who always sat outside the gate. No one could deny his miracle! (See Acts 3:1–10.)

God Hasn't Changed

The crippled man's life was forever changed that day. Before this encounter, it looked as if he would never amount to anything. This is an example of how God can take a nobody and make him a somebody.

God is the same today as He was then. When you look to Him, you too can receive a miracle! Your life can turn around.

> God can take a nobody and make him a somebody.

People may have said that your life will never amount to anything. But God says, "I've started a good work in you. Don't listen to what they're saying."

The enemy is just using people to discourage you. He wants you to quit standing in faith. He is trying to discourage you so you won't expect to receive any of God's promises.

Just remember that when the devil says, "It's all over," God is saying, "I'm just getting started."

Never, never, never give up hope. As long as you have breath in your lungs, don't quit. God is working in you and for you. It's never too late, and it's not too hard. It's not impossible for God to do what He promised in His Word.

Number Two—God Will Continue That Work

Psalm 138:8 declares, *"The Lord will perfect that which concerns me."* When God starts something in us, He doesn't stop halfway. He is faithful to work out His plan for our lives. And if He did it once, He'll do it again.

God is not a one-time God—He's an every-time God. Some people may get only a one-time blessing, but they could be blessed every day! The reason they get blessed only once is because that's all they were expecting. We get what we expect.

Once God gets started, He keeps going—day after day, week after week, month after month, and year after year! He doesn't get tired or have bad moods or bad days. In fact, Scripture says that He doesn't sleep or slumber (Ps. 121:4). He doesn't work 9 to 5, 3 to 11, or 11 to 7. No, our Heavenly Father is a 24/7/365, always-on-duty God!

> Our Heavenly Father is a 24/7/365, always-on-duty God!

God doesn't take weekends off. If we call some businesses on Saturday or Sunday, we'll hear a recording saying, "We're closed for the weekend." When we pray, we never get a message saying, "I'm on vacation, but call back on Monday. I'll see if I can work you into my schedule."

That's the way some people think about God. But He never goes on vacation. He is always willing and able to do His good pleasure in our lives (Phil. 2:13).

> *The end of a thing is better than its beginning.*
> —Eccl. 7:8

Some people may say, "God has given up on you." A more accurate statement is that God never gives up on anybody. But, a lot of people have given up on God. They've quit expecting.

The question is not whether God will extend His hand of grace. The question is whether we will reach up and grab that hand. God is a can-do God and a can-do-it-again God. We can expect Him to work in us continually. He will take us from faith to faith, victory to victory, and glory to glory.

Number Three—God Will Finish What He Started

There is a finish line we all will cross at some time. That is when we will be finished here on earth and will cross over to our eternal reward.

The writer of Hebrews said that Jesus is the author and finisher of our faith (Heb. 12:2). That means He will continue working in our lives until we cross the finish line into eternity.

It says in the Book of Job, *"Though your beginning was small, yet your latter end would increase abundantly"* (Job 8:7). Solomon made a similar statement: *"The end of a thing is better than its beginning"* (Eccl. 7:8).

Whenever God helps us, it's just as powerful at the end as it was in the beginning and the middle.

Keep Going Until You Finish!

Sometimes people start something but never finish. That has probably happened to all of us at one time or another! In running races, some people start well but don't finish well.

In the 1968 Olympic Games in Mexico City, marathon runner John Stephen Akhwari was never considered a medal contender. Less than halfway into the 26-mile race, some athletes were trying to move into a better position. Akhwari got caught in the chaos and fell. When he hit the ground, he gashed and dislocated his knee and busted his shoulder. He received medical attention and got back in the race.

A little over an hour after the winner crossed the finish line, Akhwari came limping into the stadium. Most spectators had left. Only a few thousand people remained.

The man from Tanzania could hardly run. His knee was skinned and bleeding. He was bruised, and blood was running down his forehead and leg. The crowd in the stands and the Olympics workers cheered him on as he stumbled across the finish line.

After the race, he was asked why he didn't pull out after he fell. His reply is what he is remembered for.

"My country did not send me 5,000 miles to start the race," he said. "They sent me 5,000 miles to finish the race."[2]

Like this Olympic athlete, we must never let go of what God has started in our lives. What He started in us is just a stepping-stone to what our end shall be—an end that is much better than our beginning.

Scriptures to Ponder

PSALM 138:8 (TLB)

8   The Lord will work out his plans for my life.

PHILIPPIANS 2:13 (AMP)

13   For it is [not your strength, but it is] God who is effectively at work in you, both to will and to work [that is, strengthening, energizing, and creating in you the longing and the ability to fulfill your purpose] for His good pleasure.

ECCLESIASTES 7:8

8   The end of a thing is better than its beginning.

Power Points

The devil often screams in your ear that God won't come through for you—that your situation is impossible to change. At times like this, remember that Satan is the father of lies. So if the enemy is putting up such a fuss, you must be really close to receiving what you need. He hates it when you're about to receive, because God promised that *"your latter end would increase abundantly"* (Job 8:7).

Just Sayin'

Proclaim Your Victory!

- Nothing—absolutely nothing—is impossible for God. It's never too late or too hard. God is able to do what He promised me in His Word.

- My God is a can-do God. And if He did it once, He can do it again!

Action Items

1. In your stand of faith, what things have discouraged you?

_____

_____

_____

2. What practical steps can you take to overcome this discouragement?

_____

_____

_____

3. Review the scriptures you listed in chapter 1. Which one speaks to you the most about not quitting? _____

_____

4. According to Job 8:7 and Ecclesiastes 7:8, how can you expect your end to be? _____

_____

[1]Barnes, Albert. *Barnes' Notes on the New Testament* (Grand Rapids, Michigan. Kregel Publications, 1962), 1020–1021.
[2]olympic.org/news/john-stephen-akhwari-marathon-men-athletics/209041

6
Possessing God's Promises

F.F. Bosworth said, "Faith begins where the will of God is known."[1] What is God's will? His Word is His will. As you read Scripture, you will discover all of the things God has promised to do for you.

Below is a short list of what God has said. The good news is that there are a lot more than just 15 promises in the Bible. In fact, Scripture is filled with solutions to every situation, need, or problem you will ever face.

I encourage you to build your faith by meditating on the Bible verses that go with each promise listed below. But don't stop there. Take time to search the scriptures and find out everything that belongs to you as a child of God.

You can expect . . .

1. God to perform His Word in your life (Jer. 1:12).
2. The Holy Spirit to never leave or forsake you (Heb. 13:5).
3. The angels to camp around you all the time (Ps. 34:7).
4. The blood of Jesus to protect you (Exod. 12:13; Rev. 12:11).
5. To have authority in the Name of Jesus (Luke 10:19; Phil. 2:10).
6. That God has a plan for your life (Jer. 29:11).
7. To receive all the benefits of your redemption (Gal. 3:13–14).
8. God to hear you when you pray according to His Word (1 John 5:14).
9. The grace of God to be freely available to you (Heb. 4:16).
10. Your faith to work for you (Mark 11:22–24).

11. That Jesus, your High Priest, is interceding for you (Rom. 8:34; Heb. 7:25).

12. God to be *for* you and not against you (Rom. 8:31).

13. To be forgiven when you mess up (1 John 1:9).

14. The power of God to move in your life (Rom. 8:11).

15. God to meet all of your needs (Phil. 4:19).

When It Looks Like Nothing Is Happening

At times in your walk of faith, it may seem as if nothing is changing. You've been standing in faith for a long time, but your dreams are still unrealized.

When this happens, let me encourage you with the words of the Apostle Paul: *"My dear brothers and sisters, stand firm. Let nothing move you"* (1 Cor. 15:58 NIV).

Abraham is an example of someone who was not moved by his situation. God promised him an heir through his wife Sarah. However, 25 years passed before Isaac was born. But during that long period of waiting, Abraham never lost hope. Scripture says, *"He did not waver at the promise of God through unbelief, . . . being fully convinced that what* [God] *had promised He was also able to perform"* (Rom. 4:20–21).

Sometimes Christians expect to receive from God the same way they get fast food. When you want fast food, you drive up to the kiosk and place your order. Then you drive around the building and pick up your food at the window.

Some believers quote one of God's promises and expect to receive from Him in 10 minutes! Thank God for instant manifestations, but it usually doesn't happen that way.

The Bible is filled with stories of men and women of old who had to keep their focus on God's promise. They had to continually say what He said and act like it was so—even when it wasn't that way at all.

When you are standing in faith, it's not unusual to hear many voices giving you every reason why your situation won't change. To receive from God, you can't afford to listen to anything other than the truth of His Word.

> The Bible is filled with stories of men and women of old who had to keep their focus on God's promise.

Help in Hard Times

The following scripture passage contains truths that will help you during the "in-between" times. That's the time between your initial prayer and when you see the answer.

1 CORINTHIANS 9:9–10 (TLB)

9 For in the law God gave to Moses he said that you must not put a muzzle on an ox to keep it from eating when it is treading out the wheat. Do you suppose God was thinking only about oxen when he said this?

10 Wasn't he also thinking about us? Of course he was. He said this to show us that Christian workers should be paid by those they help. Those who do the plowing and threshing should expect some share of the harvest.

We can see two things from these verses. First, the person who plows a field or harvests a crop can expect to receive something in return for his labor. Second, we have to put forth effort before we get something in return.

For example, before we get a paycheck, we have to show up and work. We can't stay home and still expect to be paid.

Expecting from God is waiting on Him, but it's not passively waiting. Actually, our expectation determines our action. Our belief in God's Word influences how we act in accordance with it. You see, the promises of God don't automatically come to pass. In fact, nothing happens if we just sit back and do nothing.

We must act on God's Word to receive what He has promised. Here are three ways to do that.

1. Speak the Word

Receiving from God is due largely to our confession. When the pressure is on, we must keep speaking the Word. When life looms its ugly head, we have to keep speaking the Word. When sickness and pain pound our bodies, we must keep speaking the promises of God. When fear tries to invade our minds, we have to keep speaking the Word.

You may have to get loud. Don't ever allow your voice to be drowned out by what is coming against you—pain, fear, lack, and so forth. Keep declaring the Word loud and clear.

2. Take Corresponding Action

Most trains run on two rails. In the same way, our receiving from God operates on two rails—the rail of faith in God's Word and the rail of action.

James 2:17 and 26 say that "faith without works is dead." The Weymouth translation renders James 2:18 as, *"You have faith, I have actions: prove to me your faith apart from corresponding actions and I will prove mine to you by my actions."*

Too many Christians don't put action to their faith. They'll pray for a job, but then they'll sit around the house instead of submitting applications to different companies.

Sometimes when I pray for people, they want me to get their healing for them. But that's not my responsibility. My part is to have faith that the power of God will be ministered to them. Their part is to believe that God's power has gone into them. It's their responsibility to receive the healing anointing and walk out of the prison of sickness and disease that has bound them.

Another aspect of corresponding action is obeying what God tells us to do. Have you ever noticed that some scriptures are conditional? We have to do something before God will move. For instance, when we tithe, God will open the windows of Heaven and rebuke the devourer (Mal. 3:10–11). But we can't expect the devourer to be rebuked if we don't tithe.

3. Thank God

In the midst of your circumstances, remember to give thanks and praise to God. Even when you don't see anything change, when you don't feel any different, and when the devil tells you that what you're believing for can never happen, keep praising God.

King David wrote in Psalm 103:1–2, *"Bless the Lord, O my soul; and all that is within me, bless His holy name! Bless the Lord, O my soul, and forget not all His benefits."*

From these verses, it appears that David had to stir himself up to praise the Lord. It seems that he literally had to grab himself and say, "You're *going* to praise God."

Sometimes we need to do the same thing. It's easy to get busy and caught up in the affairs of life. We need to slow down and set aside time to praise the Lord.

It's important to develop an attitude of praise. One time the Lord told me, "My people are not missing it in their faith. They're missing it in their praise." No matter what is going on around us or how bad our situation may look, we can win victories through giving thanks and praise to God!

Scriptures to Ponder

HEBREWS 6:12 (NIV)

12 We do not want you to become lazy, but to imitate those who through faith and patience inherit what has been promised.

ROMANS 15:13 (NLT)

13 I pray that God, the source of hope, will fill you completely with joy and peace because you trust in him. Then you will overflow with confident hope through the power of the Holy Spirit.

Power Points

The Bible is filled with many promises that we can expect to appropriate in our lives. However, we can't focus on how much time passes from our initial prayer to when we receive what God promised. As long as we continue to stand and never give up in our faith, we will receive everything we are expecting from Him.

Just Sayin'

Proclaim Your Victory!

- I believe what God has said. Regardless of my circumstances or feelings, I will not let anything move me off of my faith. God is able to do what He has promised in His Word.

- I worship You, Father. Thank You for Your goodness and grace. I praise You because You are a good, good Father. Thank You for what You have done for me and how you are working in my current circumstances. (Take some time to worship God for what He is doing in your life.)

Action Items

1. What is the will of God for your situation?

   _____

   _____

   _____

2. What corresponding actions to your faith are you taking?

   _____

   _____

   _____

3. As you stand in faith, is God leading you to do something? _____
   If yes, what is it?_____

   If no, ask God today and expect Him to lead you.

---

[1]F.F. Bosworth, *Christ the Healer* (Grand Rapids, MI: Chosen Books, 2008), 49.

Epilogue

One of the greatest secrets to receiving from God is learning to look at our circumstances the correct way. If we look at our situation with the eyes of doubt and fear, we'll believe that we can't and then we won't. But if we look with the eyes of faith, we'll believe that with God there's nothing we can't accomplish.

When you start out on a road trip, you can't see your destination. You don't see the scenery or the road construction you'll drive through, or the buildings you'll pass along the way. You accomplish your journey one mile at a time until you finally get to where you're going.

But what if fear gripped your heart about what you *might* encounter along the way? Instead of leaving as planned, you might just sit in your car in the driveway, bound by worry and doubt.

You may laugh at this, but this is how some people approach life. They are sitting on their couch going nowhere. They don't see the possibilities that are there for them. So they stay right where they are and don't do anything.

In your journey of faith, you can't doubt that you'll make it. You have to learn that the things you come up against can be changed through God.

As you look down the road with eyes of faith—believing God and never letting go of what His Word says—you will be successful. And the impossible situations that encompass you will be dissolved.

EXPECT

It's my prayer that the contents of this book will help you see with the eyes of faith and cause your expectations to rise. I expect this book to help you know beyond a shadow of a doubt that *"the things which are impossible with men are possible with God"* (Luke 18:27).

Do You Know Jesus?

If you've never accepted Jesus as your Savior, or you need to come back to Him, say the following prayer out loud:

God,

I come to You in Jesus' Name. I admit that I'm lost and need help in life. The Bible says, "If you confess with your mouth that Jesus is Lord and believe in your heart that God raised him from the dead, you will be saved" (Rom. 10:9 ESV). I believe in my heart that You raised Jesus, Your Son, from the dead. And I confess Him as my Lord. Therefore, according to Your Word, I am saved. I look to You to take care of me—to lead me and guide me. Show me where to go and what to do. Show me how to live for You. In Jesus' Name, amen.

Welcome to God's family! I believe that from this moment on, your life is changing for the better. I want to send you some free materials to help you get started with this new life. Just email **partnerservice@rhema.org** or call **1-866-312-0972**. I want to hear from you!

Gratitude Journal

"This is the day the Lord has made.
We will rejoice and be glad in it."
—Psalm 118:24 (NLT)

Beginning your day with a grateful heart puts you in a position to receive from God. It not only keeps your eyes off of negative circumstances, but it also reminds you of everything God has already done for you. Every day for 21 days list something you are grateful for.

Day 1

_____

_____

_____

_____

_____

_____

_____

_____

_____

_____

_____

_____

_____

_____

_____

_____

Day 2

Day 3

Day 4

Day 5

_____
_____
_____
_____
_____
_____
_____
_____
_____
_____
_____
_____
_____
_____
_____
_____
_____
_____
_____
_____
_____
_____
_____
_____
_____
_____

Day 6

Day 7

_____
_____
_____
_____
_____
_____
_____
_____
_____
_____
_____
_____
_____
_____
_____
_____
_____
_____
_____
_____
_____
_____
_____
_____
_____
_____

Day 8

Day 9

Day 10

Day 11

Day 12

Day 13

_____
_____
_____
_____
_____
_____
_____
_____
_____
_____
_____
_____
_____
_____
_____
_____
_____
_____
_____
_____
_____
_____
_____
_____
_____
_____

Day 14

Day 15

Day 16

Day 17

Day 18

Day 19

Day 20

Day 21

_____

_____

_____

_____

_____

_____

_____

_____

_____

_____

_____

_____

_____

_____

_____

_____

_____

_____

_____

_____

_____

_____

_____

Now that you've completed this journey, don't stop. Let gratefulness be an attitude you put on every day!

Rhema Word Partner Club

WORKING *together* TO REACH THE WORLD!

People. Power. Purpose.

Have you ever dropped a stone into water? Small waves rise up at the point of impact and travel in all directions. It's called a ripple effect. That's the kind of impact Christians are meant to have in this world—the kind of impact that the Rhema family is producing in the earth today.

The Rhema Word Partner Club links Christians with a shared interest in reaching people with the Gospel and the message of faith in God.

Together we are reaching across generations, cultures, and nations to spread the Good News of Jesus Christ to every corner of the earth.

To join us in reaching the world,
visit **rhema.org/wpc** or call **1-866-312-0972**.

Always on.

For the latest news and information on products, media, podcasts, study resources, and special offers, visit us online 24 hours a day.

rhema.org

Free Subscription!

Call now to receive a free subscription to *The Word of Faith* magazine from Kenneth Hagin Ministries. Receive encouragement and spiritual refreshment from . . .

- *Faith-building articles from Kenneth W. Hagin, Lynette Hagin, Craig W. Hagin, Denise Hagin Burns, and others*
- *"Timeless Teaching" from the archives of Kenneth E. Hagin*
- *Feature articles on prayer and healing*
- *Testimonies of salvation, healing, and deliverance*
- *Children's activity page*
- *Updates on Rhema Bible Training College, Rhema Bible Church, and other outreaches of Kenneth Hagin Ministries*

Subscribe today for your free *Word of Faith*!

1-888-28-FAITH (1-888-283-2484)

rhema.org/wof

OFFER CODE—BKORD:WF